Bathroom Prayers

Inspiring Thoughts While

You're On the Pot

BATHROOM PRAYERS

Bathroom

Prayers

Inspiring Thoughts While You're On the Pot

By Anita Flushing

BATHROOM PRAYERS

ISBN-10: 1-944662-05-7
ISBN-13: 978-1-944662-05-9

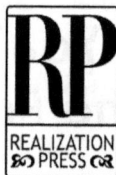

RP
REALIZATION
ॐ PRESS ॐ

Realization Press Publishing date: 11/07/2016

Cover Design by MASgraphicarts.com

DEDICATION

All glory and honor goes to my Lord, Jesus Christ. My Husband, my Maker, my Master, and my Savior – all that I am and ever hope to be is because of YOU!

To Gene

No one could ask for a better friend than you! You've been there through thick and thin, ups and downs, and everything in between. I'm grateful and honored to call you my friend for life.

For a bonus, type this url into a browser:

www.bathroomprayers.com/bonus.html

Contents

Note to Readers

I wrote this book from my perspective, my experience, and my beliefs. You might not agree with everything I share but that's OK. If we were all the same, this world would be a boring place indeed.

As with any book, glean the "wisdom nuggets" that speak to you and throw away the rest.

May all your movements be smooth,

Anita Flushing
The Bathroom Maven

Introduction

The book you're holding in your hands has been swirling around in the recesses of my mind for quite some time now… years actually. It's been waiting for the right time, the right topics…the right everything.

This is a simple book about motivation, inspiration, and stimulation.

I hope to <u>motivate</u> you to live a life of purpose and passion.

I hope to <u>inspire</u> you to celebrate yourself and your accomplishments.

I hope to <u>stimulate</u> you to take action instead of living a neutral life.

As you read through the pages, take time to absorb the words. Give careful thought to the "Keep the Lid Open" questions. Some will be easy to answer, others will take a little more pondering, and still others might make you feel slightly uncomfortable as you move outside the space of your mental comfort zone.

I've included many of my stories; some funny, and some of a more serious nature. All my stories are meant to instill in you a mentality of "I can overcome. I can get through this. I can be victorious."

I urge you to s–t–r–e–t–c–h your mind and soul; use this little book as an opportunity for personal growth and empowerment. Use it for a laugh. A cry. Raise your eyebrows and use it for moments of reflection. Or, use it to simply bide your time while you're on the pot.

I'm guessing this book will sit happily on your toilet tank for those moments when duty calls. Or, if you're more into electronics, you may be reading this on your tablet as you sit on the throne. Maybe you'll look forward to your bathroom trips now. Come on; it'll be fun!

WEEK ONE
On a Roll

how to celebrate
when things are going
well

Most of us have been to a sporting event when we feel free to act like crazy, screaming ninnies. We jump up and down, yell and scream, and wildly wave our team flags when our team scores, or, of course, when the camera floats by on the cable. We might even wear cheese on our head, or paint our faces and bodies to show our team spirit. For the "big" games, we spend an inordinate amount of money for the best seats, and we dish out dozens of dollars just to eat and drink during the game.

We know how to celebrate others and their life victories. Most of us find ourselves rooting for the underdogs we see on television and movies or read about in books. That's why the Rocky movies were so popular. That's why we cheer for Star Wars – we identify with that rag tag team of misfits conquering the galaxy.

But…do we take the time to celebrate ourselves?

We have daily and weekly triumphs. We conquer bad habits. We get that raise, or we secure a new client. We conquer potty training with our toddler or we start that business we've been talking about for years. We end a toxic relationship or we muster up the courage to enter a new relationship after years of singleness. We dare to leave spouses who are abusive tyrants. We finally feel better after a long sickness, or we lose that last 10 pounds we've been battling for years.

What we need to realize is that it's not narcissistic or selfish to recognize and celebrate ourselves. In fact, it's downright healthy! And, by the way, we *can* cast a balance between celebrating ourselves and celebrating others.

Let's explore some ways we can celebrate our victories and the victories of others.

Day 1: How do you celebrate after a particularly rewarding victory?

How do you celebrate small, everyday victories?

Both need celebrations!

This is how I do it: I'll buy myself a new outfit, get a massage, or enjoy a nice meal at my favorite restaurant. Sometimes it's as simple as taking a celebration walk – I'll go to my favorite walking trail and thank God out loud for the victories in my life, for His blessings, and for His sustaining power. Other times, I'll take myself out for "special" ice-cream like Cold Stone Creamery, or I'll buy a pint of Ben & Jerry's Half Baked. And, no, I'm not 500 pounds! You don't have to eat a gallon; just a cup will satisfy the ice-cream craving. Ok, I'll get off of my ice-cream soap box, but I hope you get the point. The idea is to celebrate anything and everything. Your life will be so much richer and fuller as a result.

Make a list on paper, or just in your head, of all the ways you'll celebrate your victories, large and small.

Day 2: Celebrate *yourself* today. Not necessarily a particular circumstance. <u>Just yourself</u> — because you're amazing, and you know it. Look in the mirror. Smile…real big. Tell yourself, "You're the bomb.com!" Say, "You're valuable. You're worthy. You're good enough just as you are! You're going to make some money today. You're going to set the world around you on fire today."

For the single ladies who are seeking a stable, healthy relationship, look in the mirror and say, "I'm a high-caliber woman, a prize to be won, and I deserve a high-caliber man who will treat me like the valuable woman I am!" Men, you can do the same thing if you're seeking a fulfilling, complete relationship with a woman who's the total package.

For the married people, you can do the same with a little different twist. You can say, "I will love my spouse unconditionally today. I will surprise them with a little something special today. I will look for the best in my spouse, and they will look for and find the best in me."

Day 3: Celebrate someone else today. Call a friend, family member, church member, or work associate and tell them how much you appreciate them. Be very specific. Believe me; you will make their day.

"How lucky Adam
was. He knew
when he said a
good thing, no-
body had said it
before."

Mark Twain

Day 4: Just do nothing…even just for a few minutes. Sometimes, that's a celebration in itself. In Italian, the phrase is, "Dolce far nient" which means the *sweetness of doing nothing.* Just take in a deep breath, gather your thoughts, and then exhale slowly, purposefully. Re-charge your internal battery and renew your mind and spirit. A few deep breaths allow your mind and body to reboot, renew, and rejuvenate.

Right now…just close your eyes and breathe deeply, deliberately. Feel the air moving in through your nostrils and out through your mouth; slow, deliberate, and soft.

Day 5: Start an achievement journal. Use this journal ONLY for accomplishments and successes! You can buy one for a buck at Dollar Tree, or you can buy a leather-bound journal for a lot more. Start with your latest large and small achievements and then add daily or weekly to this list.

When life deals you a blow, or you experience disappointment, go back to your achievement journal and read your entries. It will remind you of all the awesome things that HAVE happened. It will help you to keep going!

Toilet Tidbits

Sir John Harington, a member of Queen Elizabeth I's court, is credited with the invention of the modern flush toilet back in 1596. However, it was several years before Harington's model was modified, and in 1775, English inventor Alexander Cumming became the first person to get the flush toilet patented. He invented an S-shaped valve to keep foul odors at bay.

Day 6: For the next minute, while you're sitting on the pot, celebrate your *progress*. The general progress you've made in life. The progress you've made on a project. The progress you've made to build a relationship. The progress you've made to get out of a destructive relationship. Ponder the personal progress you've made emotionally, physically, mentally, and spiritually, however small or great.

Celebrate that you aren't the same person you were five years ago, or even one year ago.

Celebrate the wisdom you've gained through the years.

Celebrate the knowledge you've acquired.

Celebrate the fact that you haven't quit when you could have many times over.

The point here is to celebrate your <u>progress</u>, not your specific achievements.

Day 7: Celebrate that you got to wake up today. That you're breathing. That you're able to smile. That you can move your body. That you have food to eat. That you have a roof over your head. That you have people around you who love you. That you are around people that you love.

Celebrating is a CHOICE!

Choose freedom. You don't have to feel trapped in whatever situation you find yourself. Feeling trapped is an illusion. There are always options, so give yourself the freedom to choose what option works best for you.

BATHROOM PRAYERS

Keep the Lid Open (questions for further thought)

1. As you celebrated yourself and others this week, did you notice any shift in your perspective? Were you happier, more joyful? Did you smile more?

2. Did you find it harder to celebrate yourself and easier to celebrate others?

3. How did you practice "Dolce far nient" this week, even for a few brief moments at a time? How did it change your focus?

Porcelain Goddess Story Time

The kids and I were at a friend's funeral. My son was about seven years old at the time. During the service, I noticed that he was intently studying the back of the program in which a list of the Pallbearers was in large, bold letters.

In the middle of the service, my son leaned toward me and whispered with a puzzled, serious look on his face, "Hey mom; this says Pallbearers. I thought his name was Terry." I had to contain my laughter until an appropriate time, but I will never forget that moment. He did eventually learn how to spell "Paul."

"It's a good thing that when God created the rain-bow he didn't consult a decora-tor, or he would still be picking colors."

Sam Levenson

Anita Flushing

WEEK TWO

Hang Onto
Your Seat

what to do when things
are falling apart

I have a friend who has always told me, "When life is going great, just know that it's going to get a little worse in time, and when life is going terrible, just know that things are going to get better in time." The ebb and flow of life dictate that the thought process is correct.

We all experience what I call, "Tunnel Time." You know what I'm talking about. Those times when circumstances have us oppressed, depressed, and obsessed. Some call it broke, busted, and disgusted. Or, maybe we're just feeling indifferent about how our life is going – not thrilled but not in the depths of despair either... just kind of blah.

What's your first reaction when a Tunnel Time strikes you? How do you handle it when adversity visits? Do you withdraw from the world? Do you want to rant about it to your best buddy? Do you eat your way into oblivion? Do you pull down the shades and hibernate? We all have our favorite coping mechanisms, and we will default to them when we are in a Tunnel Time.

You may be in Tunnel Time right now. What are you doing to take care of yourself in the midst of it all? Let's check out some things you can do to move through your Tunnel Time gracefully so you come out on the other end a better, wiser, and more grounded person.

Day 1: Practice gratitude for the little things. Look around you right where you are at this moment. Whisper or say out loud at least ten things for which you can be thankful. It might be as simple as the clothes you have on your back, that you have a car, and that you have all your mental faculties.

We can also express our gratefulness for loved ones, for those who have taught you valuable life lessons, or even for those who are like sandpaper – they rub you the wrong way but you've ended up shiny and polished, and they're just worn out and rough.

Day 2: Take a moment and read a Psalm from the Bible. Allow every word to impact you. Realize the words are meant to encourage and uplift your spirit. Ask God to open your eyes, ears, and spirit to receive the word He has for you. Even if you're not a regular Bible reader, you might still find a nugget worthy of grabbing your attention. If you are a Bible reader, then you already know that it contains the words of eternal life.

Day 3: Getting down to the nitty-gritty means expressing thankfulness for the hard stuff. It's easy to say thank you for the good things that happen to you. But what about the not-so-becoming stuff? You get cut off on the freeway. Your co-worker hands you a project that they're supposed to complete. Your employee totally drops the ball on follow-up. Your client doesn't like your writing or artwork. You get sick right before an important event. You get a bad health report from your doctor. A family member pushes you away. Your budget is blown up by an expected medical/dental bill or car repair.

There's no shortage of bad things that can happen to us, but through those times we still need to express our thanks. We don't have to be thankful FOR the bad things, but THROUGH the bad things. After all, it's in the dark times, the lean times, and the lonely times that our strength is forged, and our character develops.

We sing a song at church by the group Rend Collective called, *The Joy of the Lord*. The chorus includes the following words, "In the darkness I'll dance, in the shadows I'll sing, the joy of the Lord is my strength." We must learn to dance in our dark times and sing through our shadows!

"Obstacles don't have to stop you. If you run into a wall, don't turn around and give up. Figure out how to climb it, go through it, or work around it."

Michael Jordan

Something to Think About...

"What if you woke up today with only the things you gave thanks for yesterday?"

Toilet Tidbits

Contrary to popular belief, the toilet seat is the cleanest part of the bathroom since most people take great care that it is clean before sitting on it, according to University of Arizona microbiologist Charles Gerba. The bathroom door handle is also a less germ-infested part since bacteria cannot thrive on cold, dry surfaces for long.

Day 4: Make a list of things you can do to change your current circumstances, even just a little bit.

Sometimes we can't control what's happening to us.

Sometimes it's the actions of others that have caused our demise.

Sometimes it's our poor choices that lead us to a dangerous place.

Whatever the cause of your present circumstances, think of a few realistic actions you can take to change it for the better.

Day 5: Go to the gym or take a walk before this day is over. Exercise gets those endorphins activated and can help you cope with whatever challenge you're dealing with today, or this week, or this month.

Do some jumping jacks, push-ups, jump rope for a minute or so, or lay on your back and move your legs in a bicycle motion. If you can't do any of those, do arm circles and some simple stretches – anything to get the blood flowing to your brain.

Anita Flushing

Toilet Tidbits

According to a
United Nations report,
an estimated 2.5 billion
people worldwide
lack access to a toilet,
especially in South
Asia and sub-Saharan
Africa.

Day 6: Don't obsess! In the past, I've struggled with allowing a thought pattern to overtake me, even consume me. I've been held captive, dwelling on "possible" circumstances most, if not all, of which never even happened. Even if the worst does happen, it's not the end of the world.

Learn to let go! Learn to release your anxieties.

Learn how to visualize positive outcomes.

Learn to breathe and trust.

Some days the battle is intense, other days you feel like you have freedom. Keep pressing on…keep letting go… keep breathing deeply, slowly, and it WILL get better!

Day 7: Remember that circumstances are temporary at best. Nothing lasts forever. The scars you get from the down times are a reminder of your personal growth and empowerment. Embrace the battle wounds you collect during your Tunnel Times. They will serve as mighty reminders that you DID make it through.

Sometimes your daily life comes to a screeching halt when an unexpected illness or accident happens. Now, you're laid up for a few days. You can't work. You must rest if you want to recover. You are alone with your thoughts. Use this Tunnel Time to reflect and contemplate. Perhaps there is a behavior or thought pattern that you need to give serious thought to correct it or shift it to a better position. Have you exhibited bad behavior in some way through your actions or your words? Utilize Tunnel Time to re-calculate.

Something to Think About...

Have any of your battles, whether internal or external, left you dead...without breath...without life?

No, because you're reading this book! You're alive, you've survived thus far, and you'll continue to survive and thrive through this life.

Keep the Lid Open (questions for further thought)

1. What Tunnel Time are you in now or have you recently been in one?

2. What are you currently doing to combat and balance yourself during your Tunnel Time? How is that working for you?

3. If what you're doing hasn't been successful, what can you do differently that might produce better results?

Porcelain Goddess Story Time

It's often said, "Be careful what you ask for because you just might get it." That saying reminds me of many of the old, yet profound, Twilight Zone episodes when a person was granted his deepest desire. Some wanted to be surrounded by books while others hated people and wanted to be left alone in the world.

One man wanted to be surrounded by showgirls and live a lavish life. He found out how quickly it got annoying and troublesome. Another man with a foul temperament wanted his stepdaughter's doll, Talking Tina, to go away, and another child ruled a household through terror by wishing non-compliant people into a cornfield.

BATHROOM PRAYERS

In each episode, they all wanted to have their way, and the results were always disastrous. When things seem to be falling apart, think carefully about what you *"say"* you want because you just might get it.

Anita Flushing

"We must accept
finite disappoint-
ment, but we
must never lose
infinite hope."

Martin Luther
King

Toilet Tidbits

On an average, a modern toilet uses 1.6 gallons (six liters) of water in a single flush. This is in compliance with the U.S. government's 1994 National Energy Policy Act. The toilets made prior to 1992 used an astounding 3.5 gallons (16 liters) of water per flush.

WEEK THREE
Rim Shot

Taking risks that hit the mark

On a scale of 1 – 10, how much of a risk-taker are you? Do you throw caution to the wind and just "go for it," or do you eliminate all possible obstacles before stepping into a new adventure? Or, maybe you prefer calculated risks, and you take the time to think about what possible outcomes could happen, but you still put your big toe in the "Red Sea" to see what *does* happen.

There are a few things you can do to help minimize adverse outcomes and produce the best possible positive results. The more you learn to trust your gut the more you'll choose risks that hit the mark.

For me, trusting my gut means I believe that God will give me the wisdom and knowledge to make the right decision, knowing He has my back all the way. Of course, we live on the earth, and we are human so not every single risk we take will work out exactly as we envisioned but it's OK, we can learn lessons from those experiences too.

The secret is not to keep yourself stymied and trapped by fear. Don't wait for a guarantee of success or you'll be rocking in a chair on your porch when you're 80, saying, "Woulda, Coulda, Shoulda." Do you want to live your life that way?

Day 1: Stop focusing on all the things that *might* go wrong! That alone will make you crazy. Instead, choose (and yes, it's a choice) to imagine the best possible outcome. Don't be what I call, "an overly pessimistic outcome anticipator." The odds of a positive outcome are far greater than the worst of the worst.

Toilet Tidbits

Germs from a flushing toilet can move ahead up to 6 feet. Every time you flush your toilet, germs get airlifted and can become a potential cause of infection. Therefore, it is **advised to move out quickly once you flush** the toilet.

Day 2: Take a moment to remember that you're stronger than you think. To take risks that hit the mark more often, ask yourself the following questions:

a. Am I focusing more on loss than I am on the gain?

b. Am I undervaluing my potential to fight through the risk?

c. How will doing absolutely nothing affect my life a year from now?

d. What would I do if I possessed all the courage in the world?

Day 3: Consider the daily risks you take. There's risk involved in waking up every morning and making your way to the bathroom. In driving your car. In your workplace or vocation. In relationships. In a new business deal.

Risk is everywhere but what you do with that risk can either shrink or enlarge your life.

Day 4: Ask an elderly person today what they regret more: the things they did or the things they didn't do. Ask them to elaborate on their answer.

Listen intently because there are lessons woven between the lines.

Toilet Tidbits

The Scott Paper Company was the first to manufacture **toilet paper on a roll**, in 1890.

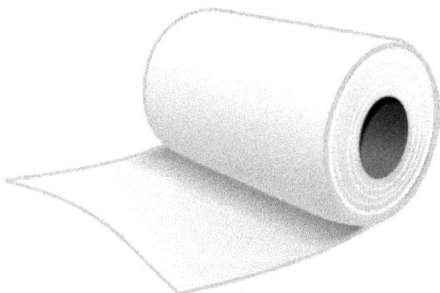

Day 5: Take a risk in a relationship today. Go outside your comfort zone and do something unexpected— something GOOD!

Are you fearful of expressing how you feel to a special person in your life? Fear that it might scare them away, or that they won't reciprocate your sentiment?

If what you share *does* scare them away, they were never yours to start. If the other person doesn't share his or her positive feelings toward you, then it might be time to evaluate the strength of the relationship. Risk involves walking away at times.

Day 6: Risk learning something new today. Do you have a spouse, friend, or acquaintance who has a hobby in which you know nothing?

Learn something about that hobby or interest and daze and amaze them with your new found knowledge.

"I am always do-
ing that which
I cannot do in
order that I may
learn how to do
it."

Picasso

Picasso

Day 7: Take a risk and turn off the TV today and every day for a week. You shall not surely die – take a chance and read a book, go for a walk, or… here's a novel idea…talk to your family members or call a friend just to see how they are doing. Don't send a text or an IM, or a Facebook message; get on the phone and make a call.

"Even if you're on the right track, you will get run over if you just sit there."

Will Rogers

BATHROOM PRAYERS

Keep the Lid Open (questions for further thought)

1. What risk can you take on today that won't make you homeless and won't blow up your budget?

2. Are you taking risks that are shrinking or enlarging your life?

3. If you're still afraid to put your big toe in the water, educate yourself on the risk you want to take. Knowledge can diffuse residual fear, or it can point you in another direction.

Anita Flushing

What will you do today to increase your knowledge about taking a risk you've been considering?

Porcelain Goddess Story Time

Like most of America, I was hit hard by the 2008 financial debacle. I found myself downsized for the third time in nine years, and in fact, a fellow employee in my last workplace told me on my first day of work to keep a cardboard box under my desk - just in case. He told everyone the same thing, but you know what?

The box came in handy on that fateful day. I was living in Southern California. Actually, I had lived there my entire life, and now I was 54-years-old with no job and no income except the meager unemployment checks that arrived every two weeks. I spent most of my days seeking work, any work, but there was simply a devastating shortage of jobs in California, or when there were jobs, employers quickly grabbed perky 18-year-olds who were willing to work for next to nothing.

I stayed afloat for two and a half years, using all of my savings and 401(k) money…everything I had just flew out the window. And, truth be told, I DO know how to live on a dime, so there was no extravagant lifestyle that needed major tweaking. There was no Obama Care, so I was without health insurance for most of that time.

Toward the end of the two and a half years, it came down to praying for where my next meal would come. Thank God I can cook so I got very creative with putting simple meals together from the most unlikely ingredients. It was one of the toughest times in my life. With a fractured family structure, there was no support, no understanding, only condemnation and criticism.

During one of my early morning walks at Huntington Beach Pier, I felt God speak to me that it was time to move. It was almost audible. So clear. So simple. I had been on vacation in a previous year to Mt. Airy, North Carolina and had fallen in love with the lush greenery of the state, so there was no question of where to move.

That was November 2010. I immediately went home, sought out a confirmation scripture (Genesis 12:1), and started collecting boxes. Oh, and I went online to see if a Trader

Joe's was near Raleigh because surely God would not call me anywhere where there wasn't a Trader Joe's. Lo and behold, there was one in Cary, and that clinched the relocation deal. I sold most everything I owned on Craig's List, and I had a garage sale to get rid of the rest. It was a significant life lesson in letting go of possessions that had become near and dear to my heart. As I witnessed my furniture leaving my condo with perfect strangers, it was difficult at first, but it became easier once I embraced the fact that letting go was freeing me from the old and leaving me with open hands to accept the new.

I know one thing...when you set your mind and will to accomplish "a task," people come out of nowhere to aid you on your journey. A man

I've never met and have never talked to before or since saw my relocation story somewhere online and sent me a $100 Marriott gift card. My best friend, Gene, gave me a farewell lunch at PF Changs in Newport Beach and the group graced me with an envelope full of cash to help with my journey.

In late March 2011, I sent 72 boxes ahead with a transport truck and with a packed car I headed across country in my 1996 Honda Civic with 247,000 miles on it. There was no fanfare, no support the morning I left. In fact, the night before I left, I received a scathing email from my dad, telling me I was deserting my (grown) kids and family, and how selfish I was for leaving. That email was not helpful. I learned later that the email I received was the "cleaned up" version and not the original super-toxic email he first intended to send. My kids were nowhere around so needless to say there was not a crowd of smiling faces, waving goodbye and wishing me good tidings. However, I was excited because I knew that God was directing me. There was no thought of, "Am I doing the right thing?"

On March 26, 2011, after a lifetime in Southern California, I left the only state I had ever lived in, quietly, in obscurity. Four days later I "landed" in the Cary area of North Carolina with $200 left to my name.

Talk about risk. Talk about more than a tad of healthy fear. Could I start a new life at 54 with virtually nothing? Would I survive? Would I end up living in my car? Would I go hungry? As of this writing, I've been here slightly over five years, and I've never looked back. When I share my story, many say, "Wow, that took a lot of courage." I suppose they're right, but I think of it more as a survival move.

A couple of months after I arrived here, I got a part-time and a full-time job, and secured an apartment; not fancy but it was my palace. I had no furniture so I would lay a couple of blankets down on the carpet, grab my pillow, and watch my little 12" TV. Had I known how easy it was for the gigantic palmetto bugs to crawl under my front door, I would have stood up to watch TV, but I didn't know what I didn't know. I've learned to keep a healthy supply of organic bug spray at all times. I'm now self-employed full-time and love watching the various stages of seasonal weather from the coziness of my palace.

I tell you my story because I think it exemplifies what taking a risk is all about. I didn't just move without planning it out. I didn't throw caution to the wind – I calculated the best use of what little finances I had left. I let go of circumstances that were beyond my control, and I tried my best to manage the few things I did have within my control.

After five-plus years here, life is awesome! I've had many ups and downs, but that's just life. It's been an incredible adventure in personal growth, mental toughness, and cultivating new friendships! I've experienced times of feeling utterly isolated and alone, but I combated that by getting out and making new friends through Chicago Steppin' events, joining entrepreneurial networking groups, and becoming an active participant in a local church.

So, take that risk you've been contemplating for so long. Grow some mental toughness teeth and chomp into life with all that's within you!

"Life is either a
daring adven-
ture or nothing
at all."

Helen Keller, The
Open Door

Toilet Tidbits

An average person uses the toilet 2,500 times year and for about 20 minutes a day. Thus, across an average lifespan of 80 years, a person would have spent almost 13 months of his/her life on the toilet seat.

WEEK FOUR
Flush It Out

getting rid of unhealthy habits & relationships

Have you ever felt the sting of a toxic relationship? It could be a spouse, friendship, a romantic love relationship, a co-worker, and of course, it could be those pesky family members that test our patience to the outer limits. While we can't really "get rid of" family members, we can learn to manage ourselves and our reactions better. For all the others, we can increase our emotional intelligence quotient, so we react in a more balanced way instead of lashing out in a verbal tirade or clamming up, neither of which is healthy communication.

On the other hand, have you ever battled through a habit you knew was not good for you? Eating too much at every meal, or eating junk food like it's going extinct? Smoking? TV? Drugs, excessive drinking, compulsive gambling, pornography or other sexual addiction? Or, maybe your habit is more subtle like backbiting, gossiping, or negative self-talk. Maybe you self-sabotage to confirm what others have said about you. Maybe you self-sabotage to prove what you think about yourself.

Alas, you *can* flush out those unhealthy habits and relationships once and for all. Here are a few ideas to get you started:

Day 1: The first action any "step" program will tell you to do is to acknowledge that you have an unhealthy "thing" in your life. You know what? They're right! You can't fix what you don't recognize.

Take a moment and write down three signs that demonstrate you might have an unhealthy habit or need to rid yourself of a toxic relationship.

Toilet Tidbit

For those who fancy flushing money straight down the toilet, this one's for you. A toilet paper roll made from 22-carat gold went on sale in 2013. Sold by the Australian company Toilet Paper Man, it was priced at a whopping US $1,376,900.

Day 2: If you have more than one unhealthy habit, just tackle one at a time.
And, don't try to go cold turkey! Ex-
tend yourself the same grace and patience you would if you were helping
a friend with the same issue. We're often much harder on ourselves than we
are on our pals.

Day 3: Today, remember that you and you alone have control over your course of action to eliminate a bad habit or person from your life. Nobody is going to do it for you. Take a deep breath, square your shoulders, smile, and get it done with grace and dignity.

Anita Flushing

Toilet Tidbits

Be cautious!
Accidents do happen
in toilets. King George
II even died falling off
one in 1760. And near-
ly 40,000 Americans
are injured in toilets
every year.

"The difference between an amateur and a professional is in their habits. An amateur has amateur habits. A professional has professional habits. We can never free ourselves from habit. But we can replace bad habits with good ones."

Steven Pressfield

Day 4: Establish personal boundaries. We need boundaries to maintain healthy relationships of all types. Remove toxic people from your life by setting boundaries that work for you. Don't be afraid to inform someone that they've crossed your boundary and that their behavior doesn't work for you. Period. No need to explain yourself. You don't need to be cruel, just direct and confident.

Porcelain Goddess Story Time

I can say with all assuredness that my mother suffered greatly with emotional illness and, unfortunately, was the most toxic, destructive person in my life. Emotional illness, not to be confused with mental illness, is difficult to detect but I do think it was the root of her behavior. Since she was only capable of loving one person at a time, I was "chosen" as the 'unfavored' child from as far back as I can remember.

I was relentlessly criticized from head to toe all the way into adulthood. Looks. Intelligence level. Talent level. Choice of friends. Everything. One of my mother's favorite "tricks" was to humiliate me during family gatherings. When I was in middle school, she would ask me to play a song on the flute, which wasn't one of my talents, and then everyone would laugh hysterically. Her humiliation worked well and afterward I felt a rolling ache in the pit of my stomach. Everything in me wanted to retreat to the safety of my room and hide under my bed. On the flip side, my mother revered my perfect younger sister. That's just how it was in our household. One hero. One villain.

When people ask me why I believe this happened, my best answer is to tell them it started at birth. My mother had two days of heavy labor with me. I was a colicky, sickly baby so I cried ALL the time. My parents used to have to drive me around in the car so that I would fall asleep. To this day I love being in the car, whether I'm driving or not…go figure. My sister, born two years later, came out in 15 minutes and hardly ever cried. Our two births set an unbalanced scale in motion in my mother's emotionally sick mind.

Can anyone else reading this relate in any way?

Who I was as a person was consistently under a vicious verbal attack that sometimes came subtly through cutting remarks and quick put-downs. When my mother got mad at me, she would completely withdraw verbally and emotionally for three weeks at a time. Sometimes my mother told me that I almost put her in the hospital because I was so bad.

When you're a child, you don't know any better; you just take it on the chin, and you believe what people closest to you say about you. After all, this is your parent talking so they must be right. By the time I was 20 years old, I had fully embraced my mother's words that I was an utter failure, homely, awkward, dumb, and not capable of much. I was told in a million different ways, "You're only smart enough to be a housewife so just find someone who's willing to marry you and take care of you." Yikes! That's so not who I am today!

I remember one instance after I had completed a physique transformation challenge (1998). I had lost over 30 pounds, went from a size 10 to a size

2, from 140+ pounds to 110 pounds, and my body fat reduced from 34% to 16%. My entire body was toned, muscular, and tanned. I worked hard, trained hard, and I did it…at 42 years old!

One day I was over at my parent's house in a new yellow suit, a size two suit. My mother looked me up and down, cocked her head to the side and said, "Mmmm…Is yellow in style anymore?" She followed by muttering, "If you gain any more weight, you won't be able to fit into that suit." I laughed internally; that's all I could do. I never talked back under the guise of respect - I also didn't possess the communication tools to speak up for myself.

While we can let go of the emotions

surrounding incidents in our lives, we always have our memories. What's important though is that we can tell our stories with absolutely no bitterness or anger whatsoever; it's just a memory. What I understand now is that hurt people, hurt people. It wasn't until I was in my early 40's that I realized I had swallowed a lie...a big one. The words, the mean comments, the looks, and the negative commentary were all part of *my mother's* sickness; it didn't have anything to do with who I was as a person.

My mother got one final blow in at her death in 2014. She had changed my father's sizable estate after he passed in 2012 and gave virtually everything to my already independently wealthy sister and my oldest granddaughter.

Needless to say that I had some fresh forgiveness work to do. I had already started the process of forgiving my mother years before but this latest blow knocked me on my butt for a bit. I was so angry that she would deal me this one final double slap in the face.

I prayed, I went for long walks at my favorite lake walking path, I prayed some more, I read the Bible and books on forgiveness, and I asked God for the grace and love I needed to forgive completely and wholly. Slowly but surely my heart softened, and forgiveness came to live in my spirit. I am a Christian so, at the time, I already had well over three decades of a solid foundation in Biblical teaching about love and forgiveness. But, it was still not an easy process.

I had victorious days and days when I felt defeated. When money got tight, I went back to that place of anger and frustration, but not for long. I know that I'm in constant need of grace and forgiveness myself, so how can I withhold it from someone else? The only person who would stay in prison for unforgiveness is me! We hold ourselves captive when we refuse to let go of our pain, and life is way too brief for that. Besides, when something gets taken away, it just means that God has a much grander plan!

I harbor no ill feelings for my mother now, and I've even learned to express thanks for a few things she did right. She gave me life, she made incredibly delicious lamb chops, she took good care of me when I was sick, and she read a lot to me until I learned to read for myself. Perhaps that reading time spurred my lifelong love of reading and writing, and maybe, just maybe, it's the reason I'm a professional writer today. So, thanks, Mom!

I share my story because there's a good chance that a few people reading this book are struggling to forgive someone for something. I want to encourage you that it IS possible to forgive fully! Toxic people will always be around, but you don't have to be their victim. Choose forgiveness my friend and free a valuable, beautiful person – YOU!

Day 5: Take some time and let it sink in today that <u>you deserve better</u> than what a toxic person dishes out to you. It's time to stop! And by saying it's time to stop I mean it's time to let go, to release the other person to be who he or she is. Letting go doesn't mean we no longer love that person; it means we accept who they are. We cannot change others; we can only change ourselves.

Sometimes we allow the other person to control us by focusing on what we're *not* getting from that person. That's an ingredient for crazy-making that we certainly don't want. <u>*We*</u> get to decide how we want to interact with a toxic person, taking reality and our best interest into account. It's what's called detaching in love.

Day 6: Melody Beatty, in her wonderful daily meditation book, *The Language of Letting Go*, says, "We do not have to take on our family's issues as our own to be loyal and to show we love them…we do not have to judge them because they have issues; nor do we have to allow them to do anything they would like to us just because they are family."

Today, realize that you're a separate person from your family members. Your family has a right to own their issues, and you have a right to own your issues.

If you are part of a healthy, happy family structure, then please be thankful for them and tell them so. No family is perfect, but there are families where healthy boundaries and an abundance of love abound. There are families where all members treat each other equally, and pleasant, positive words flow like a rushing river. I give you a standing O if you have that kind of family!

Day 7: If you can identify with having a bad habit like excessive eating, eating too much high-fat, high-calorie fast food, smoking, gambling, taking prescription drugs to the point of addiction, pornography, watching too much TV, backbiting and gossip, or compulsive shopping, this is YOUR day!

Think for a moment about *why* your habit is hazardous, then list a few reasons you need to stop. If your habit is obsessive shopping, you may be thinking that it's no big deal…after all, there are people with much worse habits than shopping. *Anything* that controls your life in excess should be closely evaluated. The key is to understand that no permanent change will take place until the pain of your habit becomes more bothersome than the discomfort of discipline needed for transformation.

Once you've taken the time to understand the root of your bad habit, it's time to replace the bad habit with a healthy one. It's not enough to summon the willpower to quit the bad habit – you must replace it with a healthier, more productive one.

Create a simple plan of action and post it on your bathroom mirror, above your kitchen sink, or anywhere else you'll see it regularly.

A simple plan of action for overeating could include:

- Cut out as many triggers as possible (don't stuff your cupboards with potato chips and ding dongs).

- Join forces with somebody with the same goals (accountability works).

- Surround yourself with people who live the way you want to live (join a health-conscious Meetup group or form a small group of healthy eaters at your church or workplace – create your own Biggest Loser Challenge).

- Visualize yourself succeeding. Spend five minutes a day visualizing yourself fully practicing your new habit. Imagine how you feel.

Anita Flushing

Toilet Tidbit

7 million mobile phones are dropped down the toilet every year.

Porcelain Goddess Story Time

My mother used to tell me, "Your middle name is "I can't stay long." She said it because that was pretty much the first words I uttered upon entering my parent's house. I knew if I over-stayed she would eventually deliver a toxic, demeaning comment. She was still making fun of and laughing at my ears well into my adulthood.

It took a lot of counseling and forgiveness to overcome a lifetime of poison-ous tongue-wagging, but I can happi-ly say that all of it served to develop intense mental strength and a healthy degree of emotional intelligence.

If the toxic person is a close family member who is in your life to stay, then do what I did...set a time limit for your stay if at all possible. Pull the "Gee, look at the time" trick. It's not a chicken baby way out, but a boundary of self-protection. Tyler Perry, in his poignant portrayal of the abuse he endured from his dad, told Oprah in 2010, that he loved his father, he forgave him but knew he could not be around him and his abuse.

"For God did not give us a spirit of timidity, but a spirit of power, of love, and of self-discipline."

2 Timothy 1:7

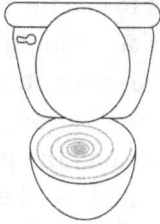

Keep the Lid Open (questions for further thought)

1. Do you have an unhealthy habit you need to release? What is it and when do you see yourself finally conquering your bad habit?

2. Are you in a toxic relationship? I'm a serious proponent of marriage and toughing it out through the hard times, so I'm talking to singles who are in toxic love relationships. If you're in a toxic relationship, what

is your plan to exit the relationship? The end date should be **today**! Don't waste your time for one more minute. You do not have to end it in person. The phone works just as well and can help diffuse a potentially bad scene. It will feel like a ton of bricks have been lifted off your shoulders!

3. Are you dealing with a toxic, venomous family member who grates at your very soul? Remember who the stronger one is. **It's YOU!!** Imagine a hard plastic force field all around you, and when the person speaks malicious, venomous words, you imagine that those words are bouncing off the force field like rubber balls. Another tool is to imagine the person speaking in a cartoon voice. They're carrying

on...blah, blah, blah, but all you hear is Daffy Duck, or maybe Alvin and the Chipmunks, or even Popeye. You'll have to refrain your giggles because it's really quite funny.

Toilet Tidbit

There are 35 bathrooms and toilets in the White House. A lot of options for the U.S. first family to choose from.

Anita Flushing

WEEK FIVE
Stopped Up

getting things flowing again after disappointment or failure

If you're human, and I assume you are if you're reading this book, you've experienced disappointment, setbacks, and failure of some type in your life. That famous group of people called "they" say that disappointment, setbacks, and failure are designed to make us strong. I wonder where in the world that group of "they" lives. I wonder what they eat and where they shop because "they're" everywhere. Ask yourself the following questions to identify how you respond when difficulties enter your life:

BATHROOM PRAYERS

Do I throw up my arms in dismay?
Or, do I just throw up?

Do I take it out on those closest to me?

Do I have a one-person pity party?

Do I get mad at the world for doing this to me?

Do I make a list and attack the problem with a vengeance?

Do I simply get stuck and remain in neutral for longer than I should?

Do I acknowledge that problems come to all humanity, and it's just my turn right now?

We all have self-safety mechanisms built into our psyches that engage immediately when a failure or setback comes our way. It's like having a tool box we pull from when trials and tumult hit our sphere. The problem is that sometimes that toolbox has rusty, out-of-date tools that no longer serve us well.

In this section, you'll discover and examine shiny, new tools you can utilize to help you get things flowing again. Pick up the tools that are the most useful to you. Grip them. See how they work. Some will work better than others for you and, remember, what works for you might not work for someone else. It's YOUR toolbox!

"*Waking up to who you are requires letting go of who you imagine yourself to be.*"

Alan Watts

Day 1: Acknowledge that tough times are a part of life and that you're not the first one or the only one who has experienced a setback or failure. Transformation happens during *and* after our challenging times, and transformation always starts in your mind!

The key to positive transformation is to renovate your inner critic into your inner coach! When you renovate your house, you move furniture around, or bring in new furniture, you paint, you lay down new floor or carpet, and once it's complete, you hang new pictures and add subtle accents to the room. Your brain is no different. What you think affects your attitude, your motivation, your physiology, and even your biochemistry.

Research indicates that people talk to themselves about 50,000 times a day and that 80% of self-talk is negative. During tough times, we often revert to the old brain furniture; those shabby thoughts that shout "I'm too old to…" or "I don't have enough money to…" or "I'll never be good enough to…"

Realizing that you are the only one in charge of your mind means that you get to choose the thought patterns that move through your brain. Get into the habit of asking yourself, "Is this thought helping or hurting me? Is it renovating my mind for good or is it poisoning me with fear and self-doubt?

Day 2: Stop blaming yourself and others for your challenges. Circumstances are irreversible, and you're wasting precious energy trying to tag the blame. Things happen - life comes at you fast. Exploring how to move forward is the most important action you can do right now. Don't get stuck in the blame game!

Toilet Tidbit

Americans use 433
million miles of toilet
paper each year;
enough to reach to
the sun and back.

Day 3: Bounce! Bounce back that is. After a setback or failure, it's time to re-evaluate your goals, both immediate and long-term. There's a saying that goes, "Forget the circumstances, remember the lessons." It's probably another thing "they" said.

After a failure, you feel like the air has been let out of you – you feel a bit deflated, a tad underwhelmed. Allow yourself to feel whatever it is you're feeling and then dust yourself off and get moving!

In a classic commercial from yesteryear we learned, "Weebles wobble but they don't fall down."

It's not the time to stay down. It's time to bounce back…and then bounce forward.

Day 4: Remember Victor Frankl. The only reason he survived severe beatings in a concentration camp during the Holocaust was that he vividly imagined his future with his problems resolved, and then he worked backward to figure out what he needed to do to make his future a reality.

"Success is not final. Failure is not fatal. It is the courage to continue that counts."

Winston Churchill

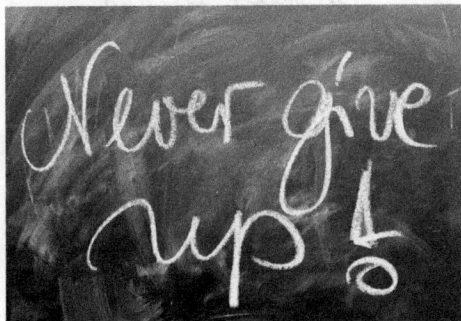

"Failures are finger posts on the road to achievement."

C. S. Lewis

Day 5: What setbacks or failures have you experienced?

Divorce?

Job loss?

Possessions lost through a natural disaster?

Financial ruin?

Business failure?

The death of a loved one?

Crippling disease?

Inability to quit a destructive habit?

Face your giant and hurl the five smooth stones of Purpose, Passion, Power, Principles, and Perseverance to take it down for good.

Porcelain Goddess Story Time

In the early-2000's I was in San Francisco visiting a good friend of mine. First, let me just say a few words about my friend Michael. He was the only friend who walked through my divorce with me. After 23 years of marriage, and a healthy supply of married friends, everyone seemed to disappear during this extremely tough time. I felt alone, abandoned, and incredibly lost in my grief. I didn't know how to be single as I had been married since I was 20. I had virtually no money, I was 43, and here I was, alone for the first time in my life.

I met Michael at the gym. He told me I had nice peaks on my biceps (which

I did at the time), then asked me if I liked Chinese food. "Definitely!" I quickly replied. We not only made a date for Chinese food but he was there faithfully that dreadful first year when I was in emotional trauma. He listened to me rant, he lent his shoulder when I cried (which was a lot), and he brought food and comfort to a hurting soul. He showed me for the first time in my life what real romance was.

After we'd known each other for a while, he would show up with one rose petal and gently place it in my hand. He'd lead me to a beautifully decorated room with champagne and chocolate-dipped strawberries. He was genuine about it; his kind gestures filled my parched soul like a swimming pool on a hot summer day, and it gave me a glimmer of hope in my dimly lit, damaged heart. We've lost touch through the years; he married a beautiful woman and adopted her son as his own. We communicate through email every once in a blue moon, but I will never forget his kindness and thoughtfulness.

Anyway, as I said, I was in San Francisco visiting Michael and I needed to use the restroom. We were at Pier 39, and I opened the door to one of the portable coin-operated bathrooms and went right in. But, when it came time to exit, I couldn't get out. I hadn't paid to get into the contraption; the door just opened wide. I fiddled furiously with the handle… but nothing. I was laughing at first, and I could hear Michael laughing hysterically outside the door. After a few minutes, dread took over. Was I really locked inside a portable restroom on the most famous pier in the world? I fiddled some more with the door handle; I tried to pry the door open from underneath, but it wouldn't budge. After several minutes the door finally opened magically, and I stepped out to Michael laughing so hard I thought he was going to pee his pants. I have the picture somewhere on one of my old cell phones, and it's true – a picture can paint 1,000 words.

My question to you is: Where do you feel stuck right now? Do you feel locked into a situation that you see no way out? You might be experiencing a failed marriage or business. You might have lost a child, a parent, or a treasured friend. You might have had to bid farewell to a dream that just isn't going to come true. You feel lost and directionless. Your heart is heavy with grief and you wonder if you'll ever recover. I'm here to tell you that **<u>YOU WILL RECOVER</u>**! Take time to feel your deep emotions. Grieve. Cry. Get mad. But then take the key and let yourself out.

What's the key?

Only you know because it's different for everyone. For some it's forgiveness. For others, it may be reading the Bible or a few personal development books, or talking to a professional counselor. It might be as simple as wholly and completely surrendering to God with your hands lifted up and your heart open to His healing, restorative power. Along with that, you might spend some serious time in prayer and meditation with an open heart and open ears.

I know this for sure - failure and disappointment don't define who you are. It only means you went through something significant. What happens to you is not who you are! So, lift your head up, look in the mirror, smile, and say to yourself, "I'm a conqueror! I will survive this circumstance! I will be stronger, wiser, and better!"

Day 6: Reward yourself for surviving! You know you'll get beyond whatever circumstance is troubling you right now. Even if it doesn't feel like it right now, you will - for sure. You're a survivor. A victor. A conqueror. Don't let today end without doing just a little favor for yourself. Buy yourself a small gift or bouquet of flowers, or maybe a meal or special dessert. It doesn't have to be extravagant, although it can be, but please do reward yourself.

Have you noticed a theme throughout this book? I love to celebrate accomplishments, both big and small, and I do it regularly. You are so worth celebrating my friend! Do it with gusto!

Day 7: Perhaps it's time to evaluate or re-evaluate your expected outcomes for any given situation.

Was your expectation realistic or an illusion?

Think long and hard about this one: When we're disappointed by one person or circumstance, is that the ONLY person or situation that can make us happy and fulfilled? Certainly not! Just like the old AOL voice, "You've got mail," I say to you, "You've got options." Don't ever say, "I didn't have a choice," because you always have a choice. A movie that will bring that point home is *The Devil Wears Prada*.

SOMETHING TO THINK ABOUT...

What kind of person would you be today if you <u>never</u> experienced one single setback, failure, or disappointment?

My guess is shallow and non-empathetic at best.

Bonus: If you're seeking romantic love and you've had your heart broken, please know that he/she is not the only one who has love to give. A plethora of others are capable of loving you in meaningful ways.

If you've been disappointed by not getting your dream job, think again. There are plenty of ways to fulfill your desires for a job that will fulfill you. It could be another job, or you can create your own business that encompasses everything you've always wanted in a vocation.

The bottom line is to think about what your core desires are and attach yourself to them. Not your interpretation of exactly how you can get those desires fulfilled.

Toilet Tidbits

In 2010, toilet paper product company Cottonelle launched an advertising campaign, asking Americans' preference on the manner of unwinding the paper — over or under the spool. Seventy-two percent of the respondents voted for "over the spool."

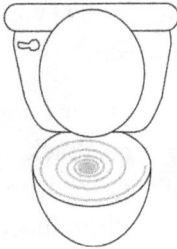

Keep the Lid Open (questions for further thought)

1. What setback, failure or disappointment have you experienced recently? Name it for what it is because that's all it is.

2. Have you blamed someone else for your setback, failure, or disappointment? Start now and take personal accountability for the circumstance. Forgive the other

person AND forgive yourself. It will set you free!!

3. How will you reward yourself for surviving your setback, failure, or disappointment? Know it's a process, and although we might feel magnificently victorious one day, we might slip back into feeling defeated the next. Realize it is a process and there is a resolution on the other side. You're OK. You will survive. You will come out just fine, probably much wiser.

WEEK SIX

Plunge into the Deep

bravely explore new territory

Ah, that trusty plunger! It can be your best friend in clearing "muddy waters" out of the way so your poo poo path is crystal clear. When it comes to living a full life, it's much harder to explore new territory when your current "issues" are clogging you up.

New territory might mean that you learn something new, you visit a place you've never been before, you conquer a fear, you take a chance and enter a new relationship or any number of other possibilities.

BUT, once you clear up your issues, you are ready to explode into new territory and swirl the world with your style.

In the following *LifeHack* article by Celestine Chua, she lists 42 Practical Ways to Improve Yourself: (I'm not going to include all 42, but I picked what I thought were the best 29.)

Day 1

1. **Learn a new language**. As a Singaporean Chinese, my main languages are English, Mandarin, and Hokkien (a Chinese dialect). Out of interest, I took up language courses in the past few years such as Japanese and Bahasa Indonesian. I realized learning a language is a whole new skill altogether, and the process of acquainting with a new language and culture is a totally a mind-opening experience.

2. **Pick up a new hobby**. Beyond just your usual favorite hobbies, is there something new you can pick up? Any new sport you can learn? Examples are fencing, golf, rock climbing, football, canoeing, or

ice skating. Your new hobby can also be a recreational hobby. For example, pottery, Italian cooking, dancing, wine appreciation, web design, etc. Learning something new requires you to stretch yourself in different aspects, whether physically, mentally or emotionally.

3. **Take up a new course**. Is there any new course you can join? Courses are a great way to gain new knowledge and skills. It doesn't have to be a long-term course – seminars or workshops serve their purpose too. I've been to a few workshops, and they have helped me gain new insights which I had not considered before.

4. **Create an inspirational room**. Your environment sets the mood and tone for you. If you are living in an inspirational environment, you are going to be inspired every day. In the past, I didn't like my room at all because I thought it was messy and dull. A few years ago, I decided this was the end of it – I started on a "Mega Room Revamp" project and overhauled my room. The end result? A room I totally relish being in and inspires me to be at my peak every day.

5. **Overcome your fears**. All of us have fears. Fear of uncertainty, fear of public speaking, fear of risk… All our fears keep us in the same position and prevent us from growing. Recognize that

your fears reflect areas where you can grow. I always think of fears as the compass for growth. If I have a fear about something, it represents something I've yet to address, and addressing it helps me to grow.

6. **Level up your skills**. If you have played video games before especially RPGs, you'll know the concept of leveling up – gaining experience so you can be better and stronger. As a blogger, I'm constantly leveling up my writing skills. As a speaker, I'm constantly leveling up my public engagement abilities. What skills can you level up?

7. **Wake up early**. Waking up early (say, 5-6am) has been

acknowledged by many (Anthony Robbins, Robin Sharma, among other self-help gurus) to improve your productivity and your quality of life. I feel it's because when you wake up early, your mindset is already set to continue the momentum and proactively live out the day. Seth Godin recently wrote a waking up early series which you should check out to help cultivate this habit.

8. Have a weekly exercise routine. A better you starts with being in better physical shape. I personally make it a point to jog at least 3 times a week, at least 30 minutes each time. You may want to mix it up with jogging, gym lessons, and swimming for variation.

9. Get out of your comfort zone. Real growth comes with hard work and sweat. Being too comfortable doesn't help us grow – it makes us stagnate. What is your comfort zone? Do you stay in most of the time? Do you keep to your own space when out with other people? Shake your routine up. Do something different. By exposing yourself to a new context, you're literally growing as you learn to act in new circumstances.

Day 2

10. Identify your blind spots. Scientifically, blind spots refer to areas our eyes are not capable of seeing. In personal development terms, blind spots are things about ourselves we are unaware of. Discovering our blind spots help us discover our areas of improvement. One exercise I use to discover my blind spots is to identify all the things/events/people that trigger me in a day – trigger meaning making me feel annoyed/weird/affected. These represent my blind spots. It's always fun to do the exercise because I discover new things about myself, even if I may already think I know my own blind spots (but then they wouldn't be blind

145

spots would they?). After that, I work on steps to address them.

11. Stay focused with to-do lists. I start my day with a list of tasks I want to complete and this helps make me stay focused. In comparison, the days when I don't do this end up being extremely unproductive. For example, part of my to-do list for today is to write a guest post at LifeHack.Org, and this is why I'm writing this now! Since my work requires me to use my computer all the time, I use Free Sticky Notes to manage my to-do lists. It's really simple to use and it's a freeware, so I recommend you check it out.

12. **Set Big Hairy Audacious Goals (BHAGs).** I'm a big fan of setting BHAGs. BHAGs stretch you beyond your normal capacity since they are big and audacious – you wouldn't think of attempting them normally. What are BHAGs you can embark on, which you'll feel absolutely on top of the world once you complete them? Set them and start working on them.

13. **Acknowledge your flaws.** Everyone has flaws. What's most important is to understand them, acknowledge them, and address them. What do you think are your flaws? What are the flaws you can work on now? How do you want to address them?

14. Get into action. The best way to learn and improve is to take action. What is something you have been meaning to do? How can you take action on it immediately? Waiting doesn't get anything done. Taking action gives you immediate results to learn from.

15. Learn from people who inspire you. Think about people you admire. People who inspire you. These people reflect certain qualities you want to have for yourself too. What are the qualities in them you want to have for yourself? How can you acquire these qualities?

16. Learn from your friends. Everyone has amazing qualities in them. It's up to how we want to tap into them. With all the friends who surround you, they are going to have things you can learn from. Try thinking of a good friend right now. Think about just one quality they have which you want to adopt. How can you learn from them and adopt this skill for yourself? Speak to them if you need to – for sure, they will be more than happy to help!

17. **Get a mentor or coach**. There's no faster way to improve than to have someone work with you on your goals. Many of my clients approach me to coach them in their goals and they achieve significantly more results than if they had worked alone.

18. Learn chess (or any strategy game). I found chess is a terrific game to learn strategy and hone your brainpower. Not only do you have fun, you also get to exercise your analytical skills. You can also learn strategy from other board games or computer games, such as Othello, Chinese Chess, WarCraft, and so on.

Day 3

19. **Stop watching TV**. I've not been watching TV for pretty much four years and it's been a very liberating experience. I realized most of the programs and advertisements on mainstream TV are usually of a lower consciousness and not very empowering. In return, the time I've freed up from not watching TV is now constructively used for other purposes, such as connecting with close friends, doing work I enjoy, exercising, etc.

20. **Start a 30-day challenge**. Set a goal and give yourself 30 days to achieve this. Your goal can be to stick with a new habit or something you've always wanted to do but have not. 30 days is just enough time to strategize, plan,

get into action, review and nail the goal.

21. Meditate. Meditation helps to calm you and be more conscious. I also realized that during the nights when I meditate (before I sleep), I need lesser sleep. The clutter clearing process is very liberating.

22. Join Toastmasters (Learn public speaking). Interestingly, public speaking is the #1 fear in the world, with #2 being death. After I started public speaking as a personal development speaker/trainer, I've learned a lot about how to communicate better, present myself and engage people. Toastmasters is an international organization that trains people in public speaking. Check out the Toastmaster clubs nearest to you here.

23. Let go of the past. Is there any grievance or unhappiness from the past which you have been holding on? If so, it's time to let it go. Holding on to them prevents you from moving on and becoming a better person. Break away from the past, forgive yourself, and move on. Just recently, I finally moved on from a past heartbreak of 5 years ago. The effect was liberating and very empowering, and I have never been happier.

24. Start a business venture. Is there anything you have an interest in? Why not turn it into a venture and make money while learning at the same time? Starting a new venture requires you to be learn business management skills, develop business acumen and have a competitive edge. The process of starting and developing my personal development business has equipped me with many skills, such as self-discipline, leadership, organization and management.

25. **Show kindness to people around you**. You can never be too kind to someone. In fact, most of us don't show enough kindness to people around us. Being kind helps us to cultivate other qualities such as compassion, patience, and love. As you get back to your day after reading this article later on, start exuding more kindness to the people around you, and see

how they react. Not only that, notice how you feel as you behave kindly to others. Chances are, you will feel even better than yourself.

26. Read at least one personal development article a day. Some of my readers make it a point to read at least one personal development article every day, which I think is a great habit. There are many terrific personal development blogs out there.

27. Commit to your personal growth. I can be writing list articles with10 ways, 25 ways, 42 ways or even 1,000 ways to improve yourself, but if you've no intention to commit to your personal growth, it doesn't matter what I write. Nothing is going to get through. We are responsible for our personal growth – not anyone else. Not your mom, your dad, your friend, me or LifeHack.

28. **Befriend top people in their fields.** These people have achieved their results because they have the right attitudes, skill sets and know-how. How better to learn than from the people who have been there and done that? Gain new insights from them on how you can improve and achieve the same results for yourself.

29. **Take a break.** Have you been working too hard? Self-improvement is also about recognizing our need to take a break to walk

the longer mile ahead. You can't be driving a car if it has no petrol. Take some time off for yourself every week. Relax, rejuvenate and charge yourself up for what's up ahead.

Day 4: To start, choose three of the 30 Life Hacks that resonated with you the most. Highlight them, or better yet, write them down in a journal or on a note card and post it where you can see it daily.

Day 5: Make the decision to commit to your personal growth and embrace how many possibilities exist for a life-long journey of personal expansion and positive change.

Kick off your growth by starting to work on the first hack you chose on Day 4. The results may not be immediate, but I promise that as long as you keep at it, you'll begin seeing positive changes in yourself and your life.

Day 6: To explore new territory sometimes it's necessary to remove something from your life that doesn't serve you any longer. To make room for new, better, and greater, let go of old thinking patterns, behaviors, people, and things that are outdated and worn out. You never know what you'll let in when you release the unnecessary.

Whenever an old thought pattern rears its ugly head, say, "Clear, cancel." It interrupts the outdated thought flow. Now, turn toward the new neural pathway you're building and keep on going in the right direction.

Day 7: Today just enjoy the moment. Do something fun today! Allow yourself to relax without feeling guilty. Sometimes, to explore new territory, you must learn to be content with the territory you're already in. I said content, not complacent. Note the difference!

Allow yourself to receive love from others today and stop blocking yourself from emotional intimacy. Not every person will end up being your best friend but consider how much you might miss by putting emotional roadblocks up. Receiving healthy love is necessary if we want to increase our emotional intelligence level. Just surrender to the love that is available to you today and it will transport you to new territory like nothing else.

Porcelain Goddess Story Time

When I lived in Southern California, I used to take my granddaughter to a local horse stable for one of Grandma's field trips. I think she was about three years old at the time. At first she was a little fearful of the height and sheer mass of the horses, and frankly, having never been around horses, so was I. The closest I had ever come to a horse was taking a donkey ride down the Grand Canyon, and donkeys are most definitely NOT horses! We watched from a distance as the groomers meticulously washed and brushed the horses until their coats glimmered in the sunlight.

During a weekend stay at Grandma's,

I took my granddaughter to the stables for a horse show. We were strolling around the soft ground, stepping carefully to avoid the scattered 'meadow muffins' when we approached a horse owner who was softly talking to her horse before a presentation. I was holding my granddaughter so she could pet the horse on his nose with the owner assuring us that her horse was extremely mild-mannered and gentle.

As my granddaughter apprehensively petted the horse, it plunged its large head forward and distributed a huge, wet, sloppy horse "kiss" right in the middle of her face. I could see the horse's tongue swipe from her chin to her nose and upward. It was a sign of affection from this gentle creature toward an adorable little girl. While the horse owner and I burst out in hearty laughter, my granddaughter wrinkled up her face like a prune as she shuddered and pulled back. She pursed her lips, furrowed her eyebrows, and with both hands, tried to wipe the foamy slobber off of her cheeks. The horse slobber was still frothy and wet in the places she missed, and it took several paper towels to get her face back to its normal state.

My granddaughter is 13 now, and she probably doesn't remember the incident, but it's indelibly marked in my brain as the epitome of exploring new territory.

Keep the Lid Open (questions for further thought)

1. Is there an area of your life that you feel is "clogged up" right now?

2. What are you going to do to "plunge" that area out of your life, so you are clear to explore new territory?

3. How will exploring new territory affect the quality of your life? How do you think it will make you feel?

Toilet Tidbit

The majority of people (53%) use 4 to 6 squares of toilet paper to get the job done.

Anita Flushing

BATHROOM PRAYERS

WEEK SEVEN

Making a Splash

serving others in a world of dribble

"God has given each of you a gift from his great variety of spiritual gifts. Use them well to serve one another."

(1 Peter 4:10 NLT)

Rick Warren eloquently shares, *"When God made you, He gave you all kinds of gifts, talents, and abilities. We call it your s.h.a.p.e.: your spiritual gifts, heart, abilities, personality, and experiences. These five things make you, you. And God made you, you. There's nobody like you in the whole world, and He wants you to be you for His glory. God shaped you to serve Him, and there's only one way to do that: by serving other people."*

If you're depressed, oppressed, or bored, the best solution is to get out and serve others. A simple online search in your area will, no doubt, yield dozens of non-profits that are just waiting for you to lend a hand. Don't worry; we'll narrow the choices down dramatically on Day 3.

Porcelain Goddess Story Time

I volunteered for a local rehabilitation center for a short time. The joy I received from the elderly residents far outweighed any effort I put forth to brighten their day. Even the simple fact that I'm warm-blooded was a blessing to them - and to me. I wrapped my "heater-hands" around their frail, thin, cold hands, and their faces lit up like a Christmas tree. To these precious souls, it was like having instant hand warmers. To me, it was a simple act of extending what I had available.

Mr. R. told me a story about going into the service in 1942 when he was 20 years old and how he was transferred to the Allusion Islands but never saw any action. When home on leave, his mother told him to go across the street and say hello to the young lady who lived there. He did, and they've been married 67 years. I asked him the secret to a long marriage and he said, "Remember, she's always right."

Another resident who had just been to a mid-week church service in the Activities Room looked up at me from his wheelchair. With eyes full of life, he took my hand and asked me, "If you died today young lady (I really liked the young lady part), would you know where you're going?" I answered with a huge smile and a resounding, "Yes, I've known for more than 40 years." He has been a born-again believer for 60-some years. I felt like a youngster in the presence of greatness.

A female resident shared with me that she had been married 67 years (her husband had just passed two years prior). I asked her the secret of her long marriage to which she replied, "Just keep on smiling whether you feel like it or not."

On my last day of volunteering, a female resident fondly reminisced about her marriage of 72 years. She and her husband married in 1944; they were neighbors, and he was friends with her brother.

When I asked her, she told me the secret to 72 happy years: "1) Let him think he's the boss, 2) Care for each other even when it's inconvenient, 3) Let arguments burn out – don't make a small disagreement into a forest fire."

Sage advice that would serve well in any marriage today.

Day 1: Take an inventory of your gifts and talents. Come on…everyone has at least one, and more likely, as Pastor Warren says, you have, "all kinds of gifts, talents, and abilities." You have something… some gift, some talent, to pass onto your fellow humanity. Don't rob the rest of us by keeping it to yourself!

Zig Ziglar's famous quote states, *"You can have everything in life you want if you will just help other people get what they want."* I have experienced this in my life. As I pour my time, attention, and energy into others, my life becomes richer, more fulfilling. Of course, my peace and joy ultimately come from within, through my relationship with Jesus Christ, but pouring into other people's lives propels that peace and joy into hyper-warp.

Toilet Tidbit

90% of women and 75% of men wash their hands after using a public restroom.

Day 2: Again, Rick Warren admonishes us, "Test your motives in everything you do. For example, are you serving somewhere to help others and glorify God, or to receive some notice or glory for yourself?" Today, search your heart. Make sure your motives are pure. You may very well get accolades for the service you perform, but a humble spirit will utter a simple thank you, a proud spirit will eat it up like an ant on a mound of sugar.

Toilet Tidbit

In the United States, toilets are flushed more times during the Super Bowl halftime show than at any other time during the year.

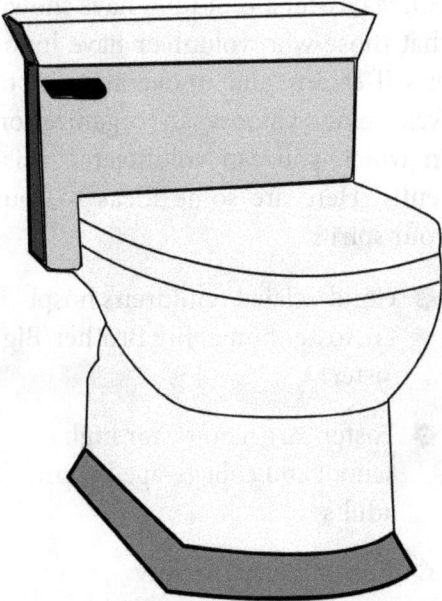

Day 3: Today you'll narrow down your volunteer targets to one organization. Choose a cause in which you're passionate. Studies have shown that those who volunteer have higher self-esteem and an overall sense of well-being. Choose an organization in which you can volunteer consistently. Here are some ideas to spur your spirit:

❀ Child-related (children's hospital, foster home, Big Brother/Big Sister)

❀ Foster care mentor for high school and college-aged young adults

❀ Rehabilitation facility

❀ Foodbank

- ❀ Soup kitchen

- ❀ Local church (making copies, preparing children's lessons, answering the phone, preparing bulletins)

- ❀ Rescue Mission or other home-less shelter

- ❀ Transitional home for ex-in-mates

- ❀ Jail/prison ministry (I was once a seasoned volunteer for a state prison for women in Califor-nia – the initial process is long and tedious, and there are strict clothing requirements so do your homework)

- ❀ Animal rescue shelter

- ❀ National Park

- ❀ Habitat for Humanity

- ❀ Local library

- ❀ Political campaign (make sure you're passionate about the candidate)

- ❀ YMCA

- ❀ Red Cross, United Way, Salvation Army

- ❀ Art Museum

- ❀ Ronald McDonald House

- ❀ Special Olympics

- ❀ Armed Forces/Wounded Warrior

One study revealed that people who volunteered over a 12-month period said they felt that their charitable activities lowered their stress. They were also more calm and peaceful than individuals who didn't participate in volunteer work. In one study, the University of Texas asserts, "Volunteer work improves access to social and psychological resources, which are known to counter negative moods."

Also, please note that some organizations take significantly longer to enlist as a volunteer. You may have to attend an orientation, get a flu shot (depending on the healthcare facility), and you may even need to purchase a partial or full uniform. All things to keep in mind but, again, the benefits far outweigh the investment of time and energy!

"*For it is in giving that we receive.*"

Saint Francis of Assisi

Day 4: Take your first step. Contact the organization of your choice, or go online to find out the volunteer requirements (days/time they need you, clothing restrictions, any health assessments needed, required paperwork, orientation required, etc.)

Toilet Tidbit

51% vs. 49% prefer to "crumple" vs. "fold" their toilet paper before using it.

Anita Flushing

"The best way to not feel hopeless is to get up and do something. Don't wait for good things to happen to you. If you go out and make some good things happen, you will fill the world with hope, you will fill yourself with hope."

Barak Obama

Day 5: It's OK to tell others you're volunteering so tell one person today. Make sure you're fully committed to the cause before you shout it from the rooftop. You're not tooting your own horn; you're sharing your excitement. You never know how your enthusiasm will rub off on those around you. Others might catch the volunteer "fever" and branch out on their unique volunteer adventure.

Day 6: Be mindful not to overcommit to your outside obligations. Your family is your #1 priority, and they deserve the best you have to give. Make sure you balance your time wisely so that your professional life, personal life, or family time doesn't take a critical hit.

After all, at the end of your life, you will probably not wish you had spent one more hour at the office. You'll most likely wish you had spent more time with your family and loved ones.

Porcelain Goddess Story Time

When my kids were in grade school,
our family would load our blue
Ford Escort wagon to the brim with
wrapped gifts from the local Prison
Fellowship office. I called each family
of the incarcerated person who had
requested gifts for their kids to ar-
range a drop-off time.

We'd label the gifts for each child
and then head off to not-so-nice
neighborhoods to deliver them to
the children of incarcerated men
and women. Some households were
happy to receive the gifts, others just
took the gifts with only a faint thank
you - the response didn't matter – we
weren't there to receive thank-yous.

We were doing it to bring love and joy to kids who bore the shame of having a parent in prison.

I fondly remember that it was one of the grandest times we spent as a family. When we finished with the gift deliveries, we'd head home to indulge in homemade hot cocoa while decorating our Christmas tree. The crowning glory of the day was sitting all together watching Chevy Chase's *Christmas Vacation*, our all-time favorite holiday movie.

Anita Flushing

Toilet Tidbits

The World Toilet Organization was founded on November 19, 2001, and on this day every year World Toilet Day is celebrated.

Day 7: Create a positive interpersonal environment within the non-profit in which you choose to volunteer. All volunteers are there with the same good intentions so promote a friendly atmosphere. You may have specific ideas on how things can be improved, and you may be able to share those in time, but ease into your role with the intention of just jumping in where you're needed.

Be friendly.

Be positive.

Empower others to make the most of their volunteer experience.

"Everybody can be great... because anybody can serve. You don't have to have a college degree to serve. You don't have to make your subject and verb agree to serve. You only need a heart full of grace. A soul generated by love."

Dr. Martin Luther King Jr.

BATHROOM PRAYERS

Keep the Lid Open (questions for further thought)

1. How did you feel about volunteering before you started this section and how have your feelings changed after Day 7?

2. Which organization would you like to focus your attention?

3. How many hours a day/week do you envision volunteering your time?

4. On a scale of 1–10, where does your passion lie for regularly volunteering your time? If it's not an 8 or above, perhaps you'd better re-think your plan.

Toilet Tidbits

Most American toilets flush in the key of E Flat.

About Anita Flushing

The full story remains yet unwritten, but here are a few tidbits…

Anita Flushing was born in Southern California in the days of orange groves and no traffic. Orange County was a baby, and many from Los Angeles were migrating to this up-and-coming city. It was a big deal when Winchell's Donuts opened up shop in addition to the Market Basket grocery store.

During regular visits to her grandparent's house, Anita's grandfather frequently inquired about her bathroom habits so perhaps it was in those regular question sessions that Bathroom Prayers originally birthed.

Anita doesn't quite know why he was so interested in her movements but, as it's been said, "Inquiring minds want to know." Ms. Flushing stayed in the Orange County into adulthood and marriage at 20 years old.

Ms. Flushing came alive when her husband left after over two decades of marriage. She started life anew at 43 years old with virtually nothing but a few kitchen items and some living room furniture. But, as always, she landed on her feet! She discovered what she was made of…and she likes who she has become.

During the winter months, Anita sits in grand style on her terrycloth toilet seat cover - she'll never again suffer from the stark reality of cold buns in the wee hours of the morning. It's the best $10.00 investment she's made!

Ms. Flushing believes life starts at 40, and it just gets better and better if you allow it to. Having made a major relocation to the South in her mid-50's, she lives a simple life of self-empowerment, and her spiritual life stays vibrant as she reads the Bible daily and spends time with her Husband and Maker, Jesus Christ.

Ms. Flushing believes that all of life is the result of the millions of decisions we make every day, and each day consists of the decisions we made the day before so make them count.

If Ms. Flushing could share anything with you, she would say, "Forgive much, love much, expand your horizons, and don't waste the precious days given to you as a gift because there are no promises for tomorrow or even the next hour."

Resources

<u>Resources to Fuel Your Passage</u>

There's always preparation (not H) when it comes to transition and taking your life to the next level. It helps to have go-to resources to help smooth the way and make life's movements easier.

Personal Development

- *The 15 Invaluable Laws of Growth* – habits for growth
- *Reinventing You* – what to do when changing careers

BATHROOM PRAYERS

- *Quitter* – the courage you need to leave your day job
- *Necessary Ending*s – how to say "no" – one of the best I've ever read
- *The Power of Broke* by Daymond John
- *Talk Like TED – The 9 Public-Speaking Secrets of the World's Top Minds* by Carmine Gallo
- *Essentialism – The Disciplined Pursuit of Less* by Greg McKeown
- *Strategic Acceleration* by Tony Jeary

Podcasts

- *This Is Your Life with Michael Hyatt* – leadership and platform building
- *The Ray Edwards Show* – marketing, business, personal development
- *The EntreLeadership Podcast with*

Dave Ramsey – small business leadership

- *Andy Stanley Leadership Podcast* – church leadership

- *Smart Passive Income with Pat Flynn* – making money online

- *Starve the Doubts with Jared Easley* – personal and career development

- *The Charged Life with Brendon Burchard* – motivational content

- *Paid to Speak* – great for public speakers who want to grow their business

Changing Your Life Course

- http://changingcourse.com/ – Valerie Young

- http://www.joyfullyjobless.com/ – Barbara Winter; Barbara is my

entrepreneurial mentor and author of
Making a Living without a Job

Organizations for Volunteering

- https://www.teenlife.com/blogs/50-community-service-ideas-teen-volunteers

- http://wiredimpact.com/blog/websites-to-help-you-find-volunteer-opportunities/

- http://www.casasporcristo.org/

- http://www.createthegood.org/Volunteer-Now?campaign=Volunteer%20Now

Notes & References

Week 1:

http://www.msn.com/en-us/
lifestyle/home-and-garden/25-toilet-
facts-you-wont-want-to-flush/ss-
BBn6VNo#image=3

https://www.youtube.com/
watch?v=x3gLeCiMJqI

Week 2:

http://www.msn.com/en-us/
lifestyle/home-and-garden/25-toilet-
facts-you-wont-want-to-flush/ss-
BBn6VNo#image=3

Week 3:

http://thefactfile.org/interesting-facts-toilets/

Week 4:

http://thefactfile.org/interesting-facts-toilets/

http://visual.ly/silly-bathroom-facts

Week 5:

http://visual.ly/silly-bathroom-facts

Week 6:

(used with permission) http://www.lifehack.org/articles/lifestyle/42-practical-ways-to-improve-yourself.html

https://household-tips.thefuntimesguide.com/2006/03/toilet_paper.php

Week 7:

https://household-tips.
thefuntimesguide.com/2006/03/toilet_
paper.php

https://household-tips.
thefuntimesguide.com/2006/03/toilet_
paper.php

http://thefactfile.org/interesting-facts-
toilets/

http://www.playbuzz.com/
ericbh10/12-crazy-toilet-facts-that-
will-blow-your-mind

Order
Information

**To order copies or to contact
Ms. Flushing:**

www.bathroomprayers.com

**For a bonus, type this url
into a browser:**

www.bathroomprayers.com/bonus.html

Be on the lookout for future editions:

Bathroom Prayers for Little Poopers (kid's edition)

Bathroom Prayers for Old Farts (senior edition)

Bathroom Prayers for Those in Midstream (mid-lifers)

Bathroom Prayers for the Stinkers in Your Life (handling difficult people)